LET'S ROCK!

EXPLORING IGNEOUS ROCKS

MARIE ROGERS

PowerKiDS press

New York

Published in 2022 by The Rosen Publishing Group, Inc.
29 East 21st Street, New York, NY 10010

First Edition

Portions of this work were originally authored by Maria Nelson and published as *Igneous Rocks*. All new material this edition authored by Marie Rogers.

Editor: Amanda Vink
Cover Designer: Alan Sliwinski
Interior Designer: Rachel Rising

Photo Credits: Cover Willyam Bradberry/Shutterstock.com; Cover, pp.1, 3, 4, 5, 6, 8, 10, 11, 12, 13, 14, 15, 16, 17, 18, 20, 21, 22, 23, 24 (background) Alex Konon/Shutterstock.com; p. 5 Nasky/Shutterstock.com; p. 6 daniiD/Shutterstock.com; p. 7 CRStocker/Shutterstock.com; p. 8 Yes058/Shutterstock.com; p. 9 ubonwanu/Shutterstock.com; p. 11 photo.ua/Shutterstock.com; p. 13 Alexander Demyanenko/Shutterstock.com; p. 15 LesPalenik/Shutterstock.com; p. 17 © iStock.com/studiocasper;p. 17 TR_Studio/Shutterstock.com; p. 18 lcrms/Shutterstock.com; p. 19 Joanna Stankiewicz-Witek/Shutterstock.com; p. 21 ksanask.art/Shutterstock.com; p. 22 Perutskyi Petro/Shutterstock.com.

Library of Congress Cataloging-in-Publication Data

Names: Rogers, Marie, 1990- author.
Title: Exploring igneous rocks / Marie Rogers.
Description: New York : PowerKids Press, [2022] | Series: Let's rock! |
Includes index.
Identifiers: LCCN 2019056378 | ISBN 9781725319172 (paperback) | ISBN 9781725319196 (library binding) | ISBN 9781725319189 (6 pack)
Subjects: LCSH: Igneous rocks–Juvenile literature.
Classification: LCC QE461 .R5936 2022 | DDC 552/.1–dc23
LC record available at https://lccn.loc.gov/2019056378

Manufactured in the United States of America

CPSIA Compliance Information: Batch #CWPK22. For further information contact Rosen Publishing, New York, New York at 1-800-237-9932.

CONTENTS

IGNEOUS ROCKS

Earth is largely made of rock. Rocks are solids made of **minerals** and, sometimes, organic compounds, or natural matter that contains carbon.

Igneous rocks make up about 95 percent of the upper part of Earth's crust, or the outermost shell of the planet. Most igneous rock is out of sight below the surface. Igneous rocks can look very different from each other. They can be white and glossy or black and full of holes, or they can look many other ways. There are more than 700 types of igneous rocks, but they all have one thing in common—they always start out very hot and underground. The word "igneous" actually comes from the Latin word *ignis*, or "fire"!

Rocks can move other places in the rock cycle due to outside forces such as heat and pressure.

ROCKING OUT

The rock cycle shows how rocks change. When the **environment** is extreme, or more demanding than usual, it forces rocks to change. Rocks move between three major types: igneous, metamorphic, and sedimentary.

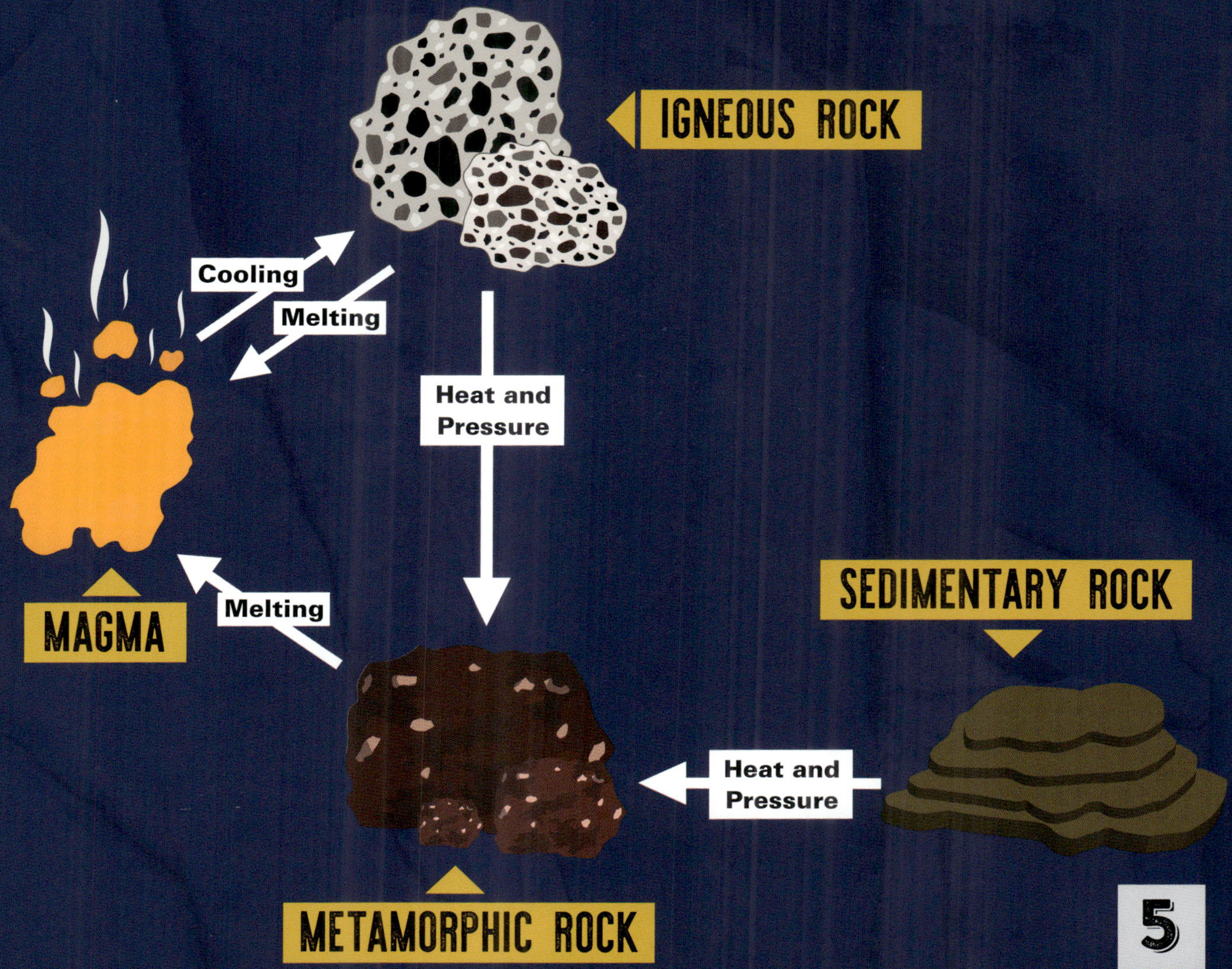

MOLTEN ROCK

All igneous rock forms from **molten** rock called magma, which comes from deep underground in the lower part of Earth's crust or the upper mantle. At that depth, the **temperatures** are very hot—even as hot as 1,832°Fahrenheit (1,000°Celsius). That's hot enough to melt rock! As magma moves toward Earth's surface, it cools. Magma rises through Earth's crust because it's less **dense** than the rocks around it. When magma reaches the surface, it's called lava. When magma or lava cools, igneous rock forms.

Igneous rocks come in many different forms based on their minerals and how quickly the rock cooled. Just looking at an igneous rock can tell you a lot!

SOLIDIFIED LAVA

The mantle is the area between Earth's superhot core and its crust. The mantle makes up 84 percent of Earth's total volume.

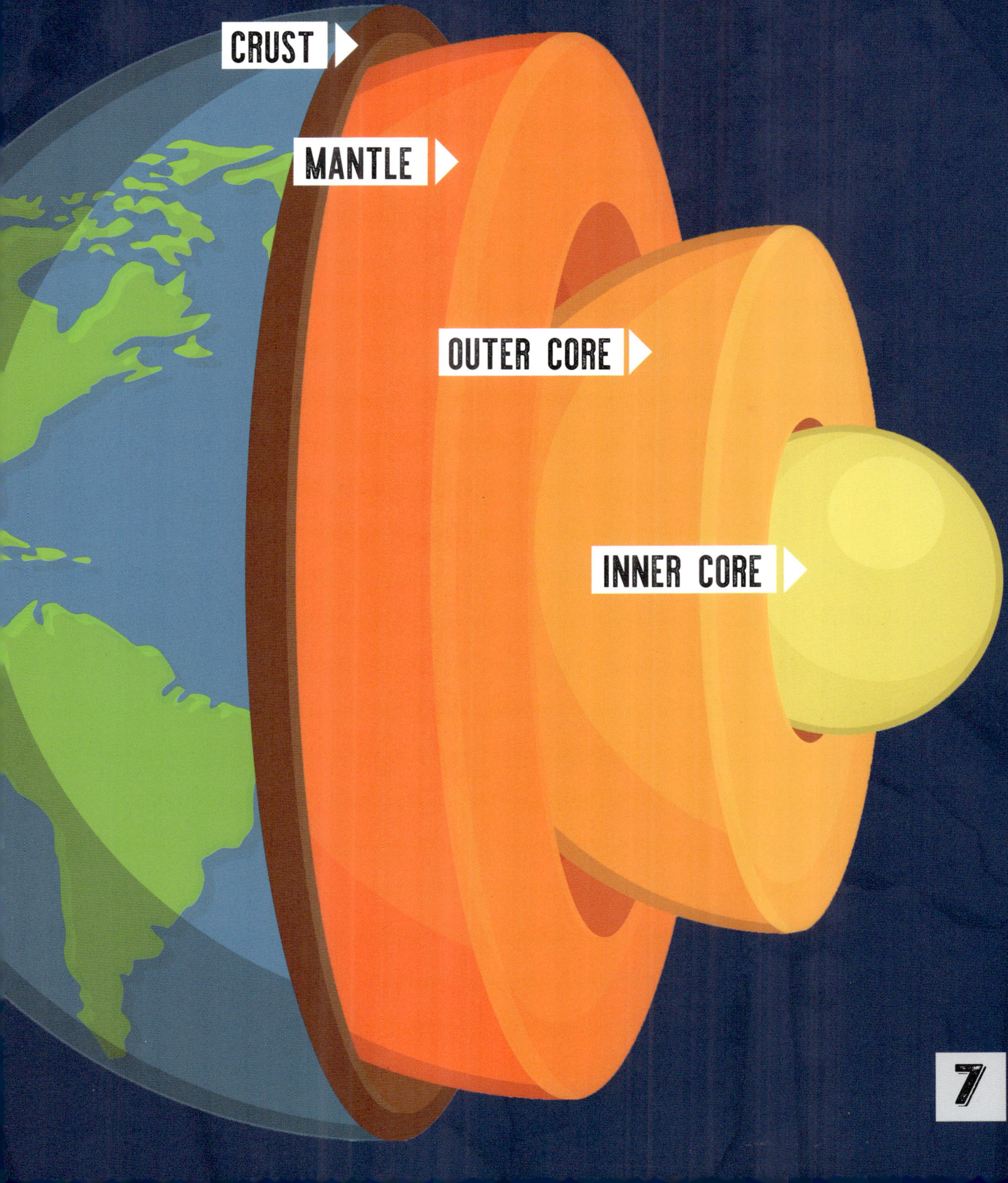

CRYSTALS

When molten rock starts to cool, the minerals form crystals. When the rock cools completely, that stops the crystals from growing any further. The speed at which molten rock cools has a lot to do with how the final rock looks. In fact, sometimes the same type of minerals can create two different rocks. For example, the only difference between rhyolite and granite is the way the molten rock cooled. Rhyolite has very small crystals compared to granite.

There are two types of igneous rock: intrusive and extrusive. The big difference between them is cooling speed.

RHYOLITE

Granite and rhyolite are usually made of a combination of the minerals quartz, feldspar, mica, and hornblende.

GRANITE

INTRUSIVE IGNEOUS ROCKS

Intrusive igneous rock, sometimes called plutonic rock, forms when magma cools while it's still underground. It cools slowly and because of that the crystals have a long time to grow. They become large, and they're usually visible without the use of tools like a microscope. When that happens, it's said they have a phaneritic **texture**. Some intrusive igneous rocks, such as pegmatite, have very large crystals. Sometimes these crystals can be larger than a human hand!

Usually, the process of erosion reveals these rocks. Erosion is when wind or water wear away at the earth's surface over time. Sudden changes in the landscape, like those caused by an earthquake, can also force rock up from deep underground.

ROCKING OUT

The Mount Rushmore monument is carved into a batholith. The site was chosen for this because of its size and because it's granite—a rock that's hard and slow to erode. It took 450,000 tons (408,233 mt) of the explosive dynamite to remove the excess rock!

A batholith is a massive intrusive rock formation, usually larger than 40 square miles (103.6 km). These form when a large amount of magma cools beneath the surface. Later, batholiths may rise to the surface through erosion.

EXTRUSIVE IGNEOUS ROCKS

Extrusive igneous rocks form quickly when lava hits the air. Because of that, they don't have time to form large crystals. If they cool really quickly, these rocks can have a glassy texture.

Often, extrusive igneous rocks form when volcanoes erupt. Volcanic eruptions happen when magma rises and pressure builds underground. If the pressure becomes too strong, lava, pieces of rock, and hot gases escape, sometimes as an explosion. Sometimes lava and gases escape more slowly.

Volcanic events often occur where tectonic plates are pulling apart or pushing against one another. Tectonic plates are large solid slabs that make up the top part of Earth's mantle and crust. Tectonic plate movement can create mountains and oceans.

ROCKING OUT

The Hawaiian Islands are made of volcanic rock. They formed above a hot spot, which is a place where molten rock comes up through Earth's plates. As the plates (and hot spot) move, the lava cools and becomes rock. In time, enough rock may pile up that it sticks above the surface of the water.

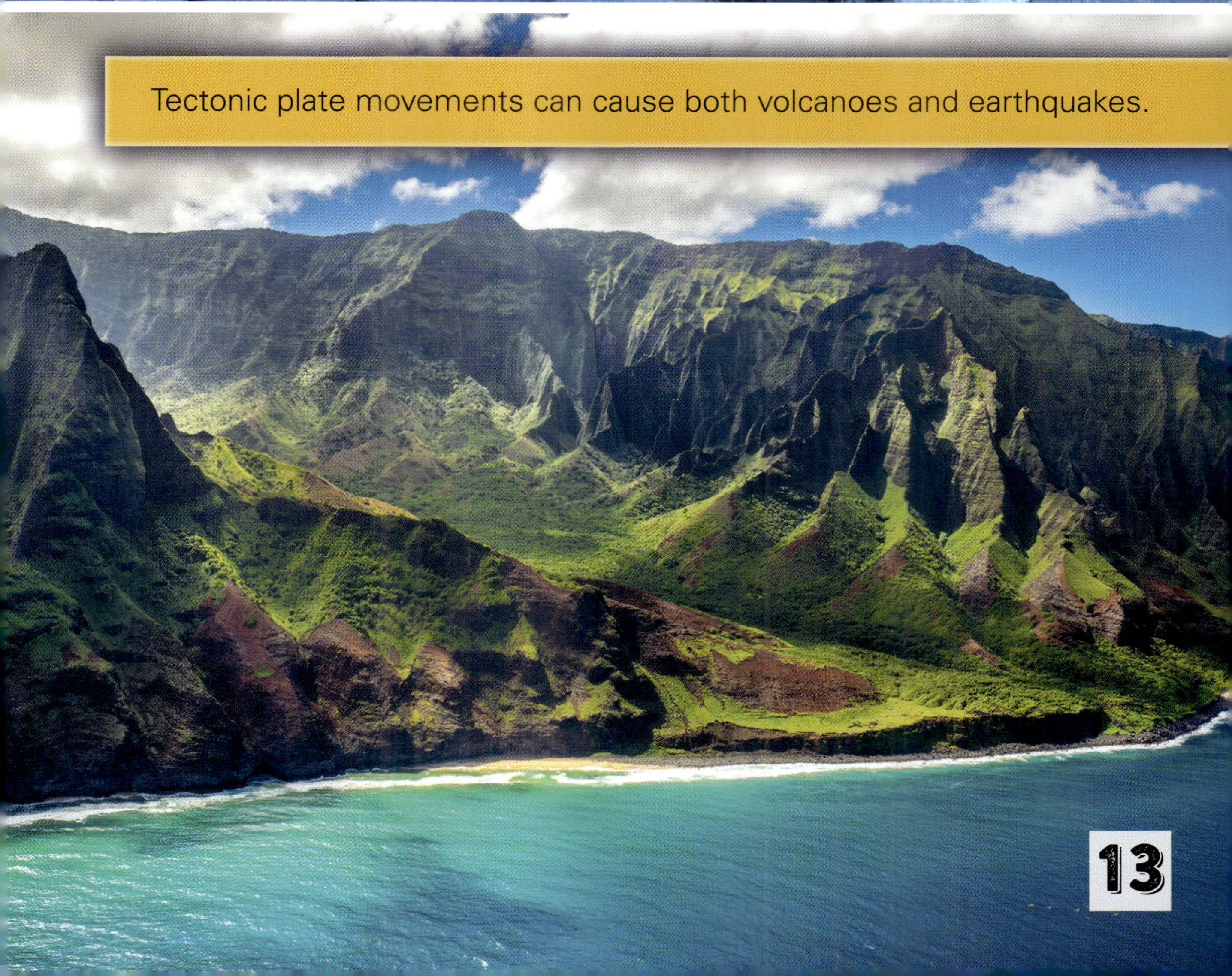

Tectonic plate movements can cause both volcanoes and earthquakes.

IDENTIFYING A ROCK

Scientists classify, or group, igneous rocks based on their similarities. One way to group igneous rocks is by how much of the compound called silica they have. The igneous rocks with the most silica in them—66 percent or more—are called felsic rocks. Those that have less than 45 percent silica are called ultramafic rocks.

Scientists also get a lot of information by observation! Scientists look at a rock's **physical properties**. By scratching the surface with known materials, scientists can decide the hardness of an igneous rock. Granite is an igneous rock that contains quartz, which has a hardness of 7 on the Mohs' scale.

Most igneous rocks range from medium hard to very hard.

ROCKING OUT

The Mohs' scale was created by Friedrich Mohs in 1812. The hardest material on the scale at 1 is a diamond, and the softest at 10 is talc. Granite is a 6 or 7 on the Mohs' scale. Diamond can scratch granite, but granite can't scratch diamond.

CLEAVAGE AND FRACTURE

Igneous rocks are hard because the minerals they're made of have strong bonds. But they do break! When some minerals break, they do so along weaker areas, which forms flat shapes. This is called cleavage. Sometimes rocks cleave along only one edge, and sometimes they cleave on every side. Ancient peoples used obsidian, an extrusive igneous rock, to make arrowheads because its cleavage creates very straight edges.

Fracture is the way a mineral or rock breaks. All rocks can fracture—but only some cleave when broken a certain way. Otherwise, rocks and minerals break with uneven or jagged surfaces.

Rocks break in many ways. Sometimes, it's from a direct hit by something else. Other times, rocks wear down over many years.

CLEAVAGE

FRACTURE

ALTERATION

In many cases, the color of an igneous rock can show you what minerals are part of it. However, a process called alteration can happen during or after rocks form. In most cases, alteration is caused by liquid. The minerals in the liquid change places with the original minerals in the rock. The rock may become a different color than it would've been.

A rock's texture may form because of the minerals in it, but it can also be affected by the way the rock forms. When a volcano erupts, sometimes the lava has a lot of water and gas in it. These escape while the lava is cooling into rock, which creates many holes. This can create a kind of igneous rock called pumice.

PUMICE

Pumice is used for many purposes, including gardening and cleaning. The holes are great for drainage and for use as an **abrasive**.

LOOKING AT HISTORY

Scientists can figure out the exact ages of rocks with radiometric dating. The world contains natural **radioactive** elements. Over time, the elements **decay** at a steady rate. These elements are trapped inside rocks as they form. Scientists can figure out the amount of radioactive elements left and, from that, tell when a rock formed.

Fossils usually form in sedimentary rock, not igneous rock. However, sedimentary rocks are dated using radioactive carbon. Carbon decays quickly, so it can only be used to date rocks younger than 50,000 years old. Instead, scientists look to the surrounding igneous rock to figure out dates. Igneous rocks contain slow-decaying elements such as uranium and potassium.

ROCKING OUT

Rocks aren't only on Earth! Basalt, a type of igneous rock, is found on the moon. Lava flows brought lunar, or moon, basalt to the surface. Lunar basalt, like basalt on Earth, formed underground.

Geochronology is a field of study in which scientists use different methods to date rocks and fossils.

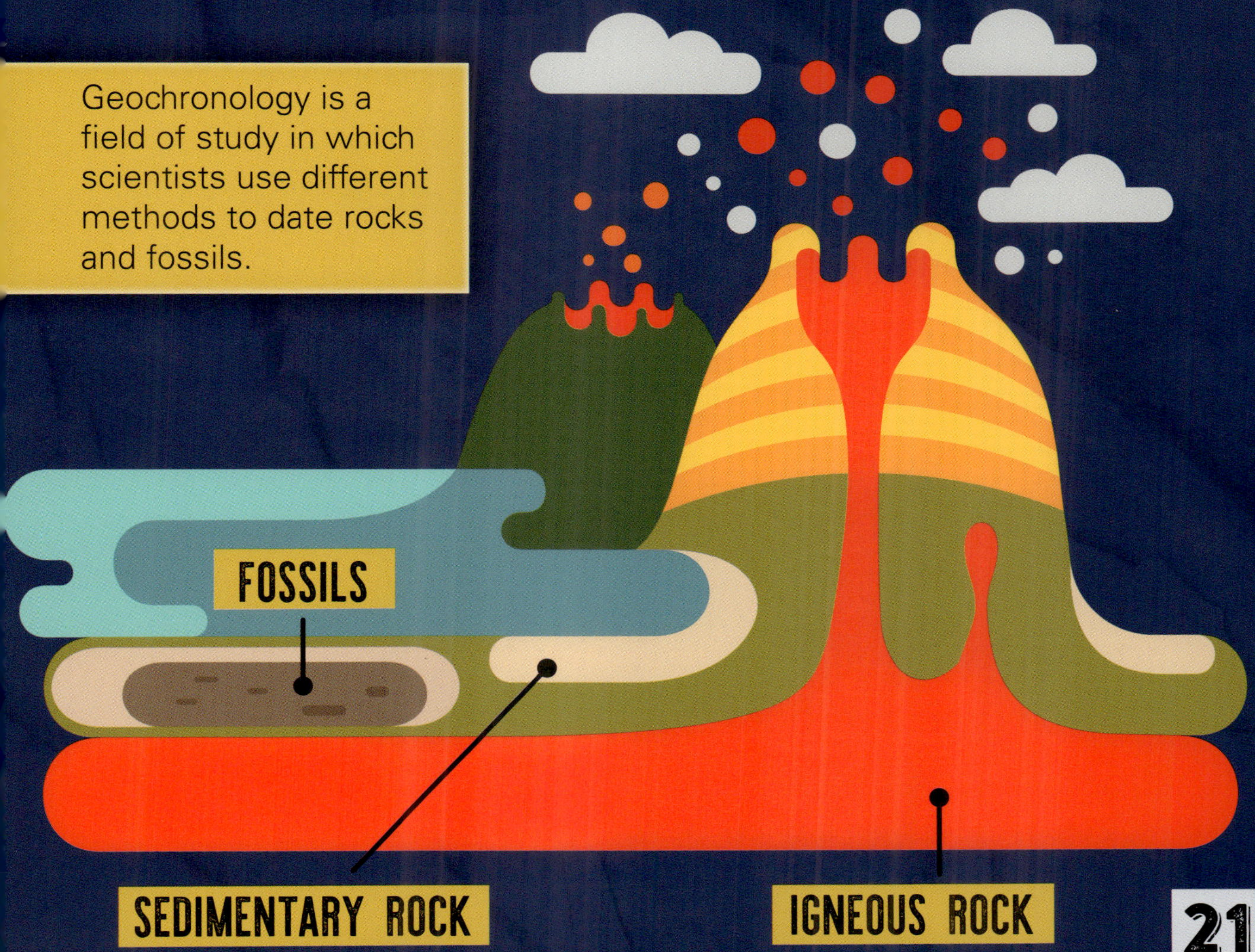

ROCKS ALL AROUND!

Studying igneous rocks can reveal the conditions on Earth millions of years ago. For example, at the end of the Triassic period, a large amount of basalt erupted from below Earth's surface. Many scientists believe the gases and matter let out into the atmosphere contributed to a large mass **extinction**. The clues about this event are located within the basalt rock itself.

From large volcanoes to the ocean floor, you can find igneous rocks all over the world. You may even try looking in your everyday life. Try keeping an eye out for igneous rocks in your community!

GLOSSARY

abrasive: A matter used for rubbing something to make it smooth or clean.

decay: To be slowly destroyed by natural processes.

dense: Having parts that are close together.

environment: The conditions by which one is surrounded.

extinction: The process of something being completely killed or removed.

minerals: A naturally occurring solid substance that isn't of plant or animal origin.

molten: Melted by heat.

physical property: Any property that's measurable and able to be observed.

radioactive: Having or producing a powerful form of energy called radiation.

temperature: How hot or cold something is.

texture: The way something feels when you touch it.

INDEX

WEBSITES

Due to the changing nature of Internet links, PowerKids Press has developed an online list of websites related to the subject of this book. This site is updated regularly. Please use this link to access the list:
www.powerkidslinks.com/letsrock/igneous